Best Bird

Written and illustrated by
Laura Hambleton

 Collins

8

10

13

Best birds

15

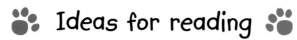

Ideas for reading

Written by Clare Dowdall BA(Ed), MA(Ed)
Lecturer and Primary Literacy Consultant

Learning objectives: read simple words by sounding out and blending the phonemes all through the word; read a range of familiar and common words and simple sentences independently; extend their vocabulary, exploring the meaning and sounds of new words; show an understanding of the elements of stories, such as main character, sequence of events, and openings; retell narratives in the correct sequence, drawing on the language patterns of stories

Curriculum links: Personal, Social and Emotional Development: Self-confidence and self-esteem; Making relationships

Interest words: hoot, fly, best, I'm, dive, talk, see, way, fast, hide, among, leaves, slide, ice, we're, something, you're

High frequency words: I, can, and, the, look, at, me, on, all

Resources: whiteboard, sticky notes

Word count: 54

Getting started

- Explain that the book is about a bird who thinks he is the best at everything. Ask children what they enjoy doing most at school, and why they think they are good at it.

- Look at the front cover together. Ask children to identify that it is an owl and suggest what he might be best at doing.

- Ask children to list other types of bird that they know. Prompt for parrot and penguin, e.g. *who knows a bird who can talk?*

- Read the blurb together, pointing to each word as you read. Model how to read aloud with expression.

Reading and responding

- Turn to pp2–3. Read aloud with the children, and ask them to describe what the owl is doing, e.g. showing off.

- Look at the exclamation marks used on pp2–3. Reread the sentences first without expression and then with expression. Ask children to explain what the exclamation marks means.